ENDURING WOMAN JOURNAL COLLECTION

UNLAYERED AND FREE

A Journal for the Loosed Lady in You

EMILY CLAUDETTE FREEMAN

Unlayered and Free by Emily Claudette Freeman

Graphic Design by Jenette Antonio Sityar

Published by Pecan Tree Publishing, Hollywood, Fl

www.pecantreebooks.com

Library of Congress: 2016931961

ISBN: 978-0-9888969-7-0

PECAN TREE PUBLISHING
Hollywood, Fl.
www.pecantreebooks.com

New Voices | New Styles | New Vision

Welcome Message

TAKE IT OFF! TAKE IT ALL OFF! That is my desire for you as you commune with the words resting in your spirit through this journal. Take off all of the layers that burden you, add weight to your emotional, spiritual, mental and physical beings. Take off societal, familial, romantic and even religious expectations; and embrace your spiritual authenticity- embrace your core divinity.

Peeling off one's layers can be a tad intimidating, but it can also be liberating. Don't allow your freedom to be denied by your fears – peel and allow your soul to re-awaken and prosper. UNLAYERED is the third journal in the Enduring Woman Journal Collection, and I pray that it is the beginning of recreating a fabulously powerful life for you. Take it off and release the divine woman within!

Emily Claudette Freeman

You got something to say - let nobody take your voice

GENESIS 41:51

And Joseph called the name of the firstborn Manasseh: For God, said he, hath made me forget all my toil, and all my father's house.

Acts 11:23

Who, when he came, and had seen the grace of God, was glad, and exhorted them all, that with purpose of heart they would cleave unto the Lord.

You got somewhere to go - let nobody take your vision

Psalm 40:8

I delight to do thy will, O my God: yea, thy law is within my heart.

My jewel, let nobody keep you from walking in your essence

Psalm 51:10

Create in me a clean heart, O God; and renew a right spirit within me.

Girl, as long as you live, let nobody take your breath

Psalm 78:7

That they might set their hope in God, and not forget the works of God, but keep his commandments:

Just because it was laid in your path, doesn't mean you need to pick it up - step over if into YOUR destiny

Luke 17:21

Neither shall they say, Lo here! or, lo there! for, behold, the kingdom of God is within you.

What "they" say is not yours to touch. What God says is yours to possess

DEUTERONOMY 4:31

(For the Lord thy God is a merciful God;) he will not forsake thee, neither destroy thee, nor forget the covenant of thy fathers which he sware unto them.

Listen darling – you come from the womb with a cry
Cause you got something to say – let nobody
You hear me, nobody, take your voice

Let me tell you this – you was a sassy little thing
Cause you had somewhere to go – let nobody
I mean this, nobody, take your vision

I sho want you to know – you cried sometimes
You laughed sometimes
Cause you had to come to know life
Don't you let nobody – girl as long as you live
Let nobody take your breath

Hear me now –
you gon' love
You gon' lose
You gon' get
You gon' give
You gon' fly
You gon' fail
Cause you got to go through to get to –
Don't let nobody – my baby girl –
Let nobody keep you from getting to you

My little smiling wonder – you peel off,
Snatch off
Tear off
All the clothes somebody else don' put on you

I know somebody who got a robe made for a queen
Jewelry made for a princess
And love made just for His daughter

My daughter, my sister –
Don't let nobody
Not nobody
Let nobody keep you from you

My daughter, my sister
My darling, my jewel
Let nobody keep you from walking in your essence
Let nobody – hear me good
Let nobody keep you from You.

Your potential is your power - Let nobody define your destiny

Acts 26:16

But rise, and stand
upon thy feet: for
I have appeared unto
thee for this purpose,
to make thee a
minister and a
witness both of these
things which thou
hast seen, and of
those things in the
which I will appear
unto thee;

ISAIAH 43:7

Even every one that is called by my name: for I have created him for my glory, I have formed him; yea, I have made him.

Hear me - and hear me good - let nobody define, you nor tell you when to turn the page

Ephesians 2:10

For we are his
workmanship,
created in Christ
Jesus unto good
works, which God
hath before ordained
that we should walk in
them.

Your purpose, your process - let nobody derail your divine experience - live it

2 Kings 17:38

And the covenant that I have made with you ye shall not forget; neither shall ye fear other gods.

Though what you see and seek, is bigger than what you have - let nobody take your dreams

NUMBERS 12:6

And he said, Hear now my words: If there be a prophet among you, I the Lord will make myself known unto him in a vision, and will speak unto him in a dream.

Ruth 2:16

And let fall also some of the handfuls of purposely for her, and leave them, that she may glean them, and rebuke her not.

You gon' love, You gon' get, You gon' fly - every victory already is promised in God

You gon' hurt, you gon' cry, you gon' be okay - because GREATER is in you

Journals in the Keepsake Power Series:

Powerfully Peculiar
Be Made Whole
Wonderfully Made and Wonderfully God's

Journals in the Enduring Woman Series:

Every Woman In You Should_____!
Endureth!
Unlayered and Free

For Individual Orders, visit us at: www.pecantreebooks.com.

For Bulk Orders, email us at: info@pecantreebooks.com

For literary and spiritual empowerment workshops, contact E. Claudette Freeman, at: coaching@eclaudetteliterary.com or visit the website, www.eclaudetteliterary.com.

www.ingramcontent.com/pod-product-compliance
Lightning Source LLC
LaVergne TN
LVHW051523080426
835509LV00017B/2181